W9-BUP-940

Martha's Vineyard

GARDENS AND HOUSES

Martha's Vineyard

GARDENS AND HOUSES

PHOTOGRAPHY BY TAYLOR LEWIS

TEXT BY CATHERINE FALLIN AND ELIZABETH TALBOT

Simon and Schuster

NEW YORK LONDON TORONTO SYDNEY TOKYO SINGAPORE

SIMON & SCHUSTER
Simon & Schuster Building
Rockefeller Center
1230 Avenue of the Americas
New York, New York 10020

Copyright © 1992 Taylor Lewis and Catherine Fallin

All rights reserved including the right of reproduction in whole or in part in any form.

SIMON & SCHUSTER and colophon are registered trademarks of Simon & Schuster Inc.

Designed by Taylor Lewis and Abby Kagan
Printed in Singapore

2   4   6   8   10   9   7   5   3   1

Library of Congress Cataloging-in-Publication Data

Lewis, Taylor Biggs.
Martha's Vineyard gardens and houses / photography by Taylor Lewis;
text by Catherine Fallin and Elizabeth Talbot.
p.   cm.
ISBN 0-671-75858-6 : $45.00
1. Martha's Vineyard (Mass.)—Description and travel—Views.
2. Dwellings—Massachusetts—Martha's Vineyard—Pictorial works.
3. Gardens—Massachusetts—Martha's Vineyard—Pictorial works.
I. Fallin, Catherine. II. Talbot, Elizabeth (Elizabeth Speakman)
III. Title.
F72.M5L49   1992   91-40457
779'.9974494—dc20   CIP

ISBN: 0-671-75858-6

Acknowledgments

To the homeowners who so generously opened their homes and gardens and allowed us to share a very private and personal part of their lives in photographing and writing about them. To architect Joe Eldredge for introducing us to special places and people around the Island, and without whose boundless energy and enthusiasm for our project this book would not have been the same. To Anne Hale for her suggestions about wonderful gardens and for her good will and interest in our whole project. To Justine Priestley and Arthur Smadbeck for so good-humoredly fielding our packages and messages. To Joan Wuerth, Jan Cable, Annajean Brown, Margaret R. Steele, John A. Blair, Judith E. Federowicz, Stan Hart, and Ruth Dolby for suggestions of houses to see and recent historical facts. To Josephine Bruno, Dot Howard, and Ellie Kranz for garden suggestions; to Brendan O'Neil for his insights into Island history, historic houses and sites. Also thanks to Anne C. Allen for her help in verification of facts and Island history. To Robert Douglas for letting us board the *Shenandoah* to photograph and William Marks of VERI for allowing us to photograph the East Chop Light. Special thanks to Sue Pressman for connecting the three of us. To Pat Brienen, our agent, and Patty Leasure, our editor, for their constant support and encouragement as well as thoughtful suggestions.

To Greg Hadley, our photography assistant, who once again never flagged in his photographic work, for taking care of the many details of our work—sorting, filing, checking, recording, checking again, ordering film, and generally keeping track of the detritus of our lives.

To our freelance support staff for all their help and caring well beyond the bounds of duty and to whom enough credit can never be given: designer Abby Kagan for her extra careful preparation of dummy and mechanicals; copy editors Kate Scott and Marion Baker; Pamela Stinson for checking the dummy and mechanicals; Susan Groarke not only for proofreading but also juggling all the last minute corrections; Pauline Piekarz for proofreading; Greg Goebel for filling in as photography assistant.

To an island we fell in love with when we arrived by ferry from Nantucket one summer and decided to try to capture in photographs and words what we saw and felt. After living and working there for half a year, we will never leave for long. It just keeps getting better.

INTRODUCTION

Martha's Vineyard, a few miles off the shores of Cape Cod, was formed by the glacier that shaped the New England coastline from the ragged coast of Maine to Long Island, including Cape Cod and Nantucket.

The Vineyard's topography is the most varied. It is as if the glacier outdid itself to put all possible variations into this one small place. Of course, it is more scientific than that: Martha's Vineyard was at the edge of the glacier and was formed by its terminal moraine and outwash plains. As the glacier retreated, it left large boulders and rocks along with various other debris. It sculpted the harbors of Edgartown, Oak Bluffs, Vineyard Haven, and Menemsha; the Island's bays and ponds, some of which are salt water, others fresh.

On the Island, vast expanses of sea and sky give way to wooded coves, fingers of land and deep estuaries, salt marsh, sandy beaches, rock-strewn Atlantic coast, and the famous multi-colored cliffs at Gay Head whose deposits of three geologic periods, exposed and rearranged in the Pleistocene glaciation, may be the largest in the world. In the middle of the island are vast forests, wild moors, pastures for sheep and cattle. Roads and tree-covered lanes are lined with stone walls that hint of the mountains of central New England. A turn down a lane or over the rise of a hill suddenly affords a glimpse of a sheltered cove or glorious coastline.

The Island is divided into Up-Island and Down-Island, referring not to north or south, but rather the nautical use of up and down the longitude lines: up is west, or away from the prime meridian, and down is east, or toward it. The Island has always been in partnership with the sea, its inhabitants' livelihoods fishing, sailing, and shipbuilding. Once a major haven for trading vessels on the route from Boston to New York or the West Indies, it has more recently become a retreat for pleasure craft and summer holidays.

Down-island contains the large towns of Edgartown, Oak Bluffs, and Vineyard Haven and the attendant points in between. Up-island includes West Tisbury, Chilmark, Menemsha, and Gay Head, in addition to little villages, farms, and clusters of houses along the coast. If you are down-island, you might be in Edgartown, the oldest of the towns, settled in 1642 by Thomas Mayhew and others to whom he granted or sold pieces of land. Made up of fishermen, seamen, and craftsmen, Edgartown was pretty much like many another coastal New England settlement of the first half of the seventeenth century. Whaling was part of the industry from the beginning, done from shore in small craft until after the Revolution. Then the whales were becoming scarcer, which meant going increasingly farther to sea, eventually to the Far East, on voyages of up to several years. It was then that the masters really became wealthy and the grand homes were built on the Island.

Vineyard Haven, on the north shore, was settled by two families from up-island in West Tisbury, the Chases and the Wests, in 1674 and 1682 respectively. By the late seventeenth and early eighteenth century, there were thirty or so families and their descendants who were established on the Vineyard.

Oak Bluffs is the most recent of any of the towns on the Island. It has long been an integrated community settled by prominent black and white families of New England—the summer home of judges and politicians, doctors and lawyers, artists, writers, musicians, and actors. An early example of a planned community, Oak Bluffs has parks, exquisite little Victorian campground cottages, grand Victorian houses along the seaside and Ocean Park, and the later large shingle-style Victorian summer houses in East Chop.

Up-island is much less populated, but was actully part of the early settlement of the Island. Music Street in West Tisbury and Tea Lane in Chilmark have some of the oldest houses on the Island as do Indian Hill, Menemsha, and Cedar Tree Neck. Farmers and seamen settled this part of the Island. A high mid-seventeenth-century stone wall that crosses the Island in Chilmark is said to have been built to divide the white settlers' land from the Indians'. The Wampanoag Indians, part of the extended Algonquin group, were, of course, the true settlers of the Island. A friendly tribe with a well-established culture when the English arrived, they were fishermen and farmers, seamen and hunters, killing whales for meat from dugout canoes. These Native Americans were all but wiped out by the European diseases of smallpox and diphtheria, to which they had no resistance. The town of Gay Head is partially populated by the Wampanoags, who have recently been granted tribal recognition by the federal government and reclamation of some 400 acres of their common land in Gay Head. Portuguese seamen and whalemen were also prominent in the early settlement of the Vineyard well before the American Revolution.

As are all islands and coastline, Martha's Vineyard is a fragile outpost of land that must be protected from erosion and over-population. Its wetlands, meadows, and forests are home to a multitude of plant and animal wildlife communities. Conservation and preservation of the Island's resources and history are protected by many active and effective groups on the Island. The Vineyard Conservation Society and the Martha's Vineyard Land Bank actively acquire land. Approximately 12,000 acres, which comprises about 18% of the Island, is now restricted from development and held for public use. The Vineyard Open Land Foundation and the Martha's Vineyard Commission are involved in land planning. Other important groups that preserve and protect the Island are the Martha's Vineyard Garden Club, the Sheriff's Meadow Foundation, the Trustees of Reservations, Felix Neck Wildlife Refuge, Dukes County Historical Society, and Martha's Vineyard Historical Preservation Society as well as Vineyard Environmental Research Institute, which owns and maintains some of the Island's historic lighthouses.

Most people think of Martha's Vineyard as a summer island, and it is indeed wonderful then, with long summer days and warm nights. Sea breezes gently cool the air; fragrant wild shrubs and trees burst into bloom in spring, which might arrive the first of March or not until well into April. The air smells of pine forests, new-mown hay, honeysuckle, sweet pepper bush, swamp azaleas, and more. Abundant fruit trees, wild berry bushes, beach plums that are native to a very small part of the New England coast, and, of course, wild grapes of a score of varieties—all grow in profusion. Early summer and fall are marked by sparkling clear days. Winter is cold and rainy, and sometimes blizzards and northeasters cover the island in a thick blanket of snow. Though more temperate than much of New England because the climate is moderated by the surrounding sea and sheltered from the cold Labrador currents by Cape Cod, the Island is still very much part of that geographic region with its grand and sometimes bleak winters.

Physically Martha's Vineyard is many places, but its character is best defined by the people who live here, whether year-round or only part of the year. Definitely New England in personality, flavored with Yankee ingenuity, self-reliance, and independence, its residents are from all over the world. There is a very strong sense of community on the Vineyard as well as a great diversity of life-styles and professions. There are six towns on the Island and each one is a devoutly individual community of its own. Vineyard summer residents are just as diverse and dedicated to the Island as any year-rounder, whether their families have been coming here for five generations or one. Each summer visitor discovers a different island, since everyone seeks a different kind of refuge. And it is possible to find seclusion in a cottage down a long, windy lane far away from town but close to the water—for you are never far from water on the Island—or lively and stimulating conversation in the heart of a thriving summer community.

This book is about the Island and its homes and gardens; therefore, it is also about the people of the Vineyard. An individual's home and garden reveal both a private and public expression of self. Whether we have designed them ourselves or have bought a house built for someone else and interpreted and changed it to suit our needs, our home and garden reflect the way we shelter our family and friends and, most of all, ourselves. Nothing can describe the individualism of Martha's Vineyard more than this markedly diverse sampling of gardens and homes gathered here in photographs and words. A combination of Taylor Lewis's excitement and expertise with the visual charisma of the architecture and gardens, Catherine Fallin's fascination with the why and how of creating the magnetism of the place, and Elizabeth Talbot's long association and deep love of the Island and its most special places, this book is about the allure of this unique outpost at sea.

DOWN-ISLAND

This house known as Pineapple House is one of the oldest in Edgartown. The lot was purchased from Governor Thomas Mayhew in 1679 by John Coffin, son of Tristram Coffin, one of the early settlers of Nantucket. Built soon after 1682, when John Coffin came to Edgartown, the original house was 24 feet wide by 32 feet deep and consisted of two stories plus a basement on the front and one story on the back. The front of the house faced the harbor, as did all the houses at that time, since there was no street behind them until much later. The land slopes down to the water, so the first floor on what is now the street side is the second floor on the water side. John Coffin was a blacksmith by trade, and his shop was in the lower level of the house. Several subsequent owners in the 1700's were also tradesmen. Among them were a cooper, a shoemaker, and a tailor.

The present house is a much expanded version of the original; the dining room and porch wing of the house were added around 1877. The current owners, Paul and Jacquelyn Ronan, have done extensive restorations and have furnished the house with a combination of antiques, some found in it, others purchased elsewhere on the Island.

The Georgian front was probably added around 1786, when South Water Street was laid out. Boxwood hedges line the brick front walk and privet outlines the property edges. Perennial borders and roses are planted selectively throughout the property's extensive lawns.

RIGHT: *The cozy den, overlooking the harbor, is furnished with wool-on-cotton crewel-upholstered chairs and sofa and period tables and side chairs. The Windsor chair is next to a period Chippendale tiger-maple drop-leaf table that holds a pair of turned wooden candlestick lamps and an early American pewter pitcher. The lithographs to the right of the window are of eighteenth-century English gentlemen and were found in the house. A tole tea-canister lamp sits on the corner table. In front of the sofa is a camphor tea chest that came around the Horn on a sailing vessel.*

ABOVE: *A ship's inclinometer sits above the doorway leading from the den to the hall. The original entrance to the house on the water side is to the right. The mural painted on the wall above the chair rail is of the Inner Harbor in all seasons, as seen from the Ronans' front porch. The railing along the bottom of the mural is the Ronans' porch railing. The white stair rail on the left belongs to the narrow, steep stairs that lead to the second floor.*

ABOVE: *Beneath the peak of the newly raised kitchen ceiling is a ship's figurehead, ca. 1750, that was inherited with the house. It had originally been on the barn across the street.*

LEFT: *The kitchen—breakfast room extension and sun porch have recently been added on to the old kitchen. The ceiling was taken out to expose the roof beams. The spectacular view of the Inner Harbor through the breakfast-room window includes the Reading Room, a private club, situated on a long pier. Tower Hill can be seen through the windows on the right.*

ABOVE: *A view of the rear of the house shows the extensive lawns between it and the water. Even though the original house was modest in size, it occupied a commanding position on the hill above the harbor. This viewpoint shows the morning room above the porch on the left and the new kitchen and sun porch addition on the right. The ground-level patio can be reached from the original basement by going down a few steps. Stone retaining walls across the back of the house hold beds of perennials.*

RIGHT: *Cirrus clouds in the clear blue sky are characteristic of the cool June days that are so enticing on Martha's Vineyard. The stark white chairs, railing, and umbrella lend an almost surrealistic look to the deck, a good vantage point to observe the activity of the Inner Harbor.*

NOAH'S ARK

 The house at 72 North Water Street is one in a row of Greek Revival houses typical of those built for the whaling captains of Edgartown in the first half of the nineteenth century, when the whaling ships brought the town to its peak of prosperity. The houses are skewed to the street but parallel to their lot lines. Since they face Cape Pogue, tradition has it that they were positioned toward the direction of the returning ships. Many of these houses that sit so close together have extensive rear gardens, and number 72, owned by Douglas and Lorna Garron, is no exception. The garden was designed in the late 1920's for Lorna's grandmother by her great-uncle (her grandmother's brother), Arthur Underhill, a professional landscape gardener in New York and New Jersey. He planned a number of gardens in Edgartown during that period.

In the spring the garden is filled with the pinks, blues, whites, and yellows that were common in Colonial gardens. Lorna has chosen the old-fashioned flowers for their colors in the spring. In July the borders are filled with daylilies (*Hemerocallis* hybrids), white phlox (*Phlox paniculata*), and globe thistles (*Echinops ritro*).

ABOVE: *The back of the house as seen from the rear of the garden. In the foreground a bed of hostas is just inside the covered garden gate. The path leads into the inner garden, encircled with perennial beds.* RIGHT: *An overview of the garden from the second-floor porch. The giant boxwood were originally four plants but, since the 1920's, they have grown together into two giant shrubs. In the far right corner are a Chinese dogwood (Cornus kousa) and a late-flowering Viburnum 'Americana.'* BELOW: *In this inviting corner of the garden, lemon-yellow and orange daylilies are backed by vibrant blue globe thistles. Interspersed around the border are white and rose-colored phlox, Nicotiana alata, and coral bells (Heuchera hybrid).*

ON THE WATERFRONT

Across the street from grand Greek Revival houses built for the whaling masters of Edgartown is this eccentric gray-shingled house. Located between North Water Street and Edgartown Harbor, it began in 1832 as a general provisions store operated by the Pease brothers. Rumor has it that the lower floor, which is below ground on the street side and on ground level on the water side, was once a tavern. In the early part of the twentieth century there was a coal wharf just below the house.

The onetime entrance to the store on North Water Street now opens into the back of the house near the kitchen. No one knows just how many additions were made or when, but it is apparent from the arrangement of doors, windows, and stairway inside that there have been several. Around the turn of the century, the house was a grand Victorian structure, complete with sweeping lawns and a large formal garden hidden from the street by high privet hedges.

When Jayne and Frank Ikard purchased the house in 1981, they restored and refurbished it, lightening up the dark downstairs rooms by painting all the walls white. They widened doorways and rearranged rooms and walls to open the house to harbor views wherever possible.

RIGHT: *The bright dining room is highlighted with the bold oil paintings of Vineyard artist Michael O'Shaughnessy. The large oak table was in the house when the Ikards purchased it; when all the leaves are added the table can seat twenty comfortably. A few steps down from the dining room is the large living room. The painting on the wall to the left of the doors out to the deck was painted by Island artist Stanley Murphy.*

LEFT: *Seen from the harbor's edge, the house shows three full floors, while there are only two on the street side. On either side can be seen the Greek Revival dwellings that line the other side of South Water Street.*

RIGHT: **The deck outside the living room has an impressive view of all the activities of Edgartown Harbor.**

LEFT: *The main entrance to the house is through the dining room.*

RIGHT: *The kitchen underwent the most dramatic changes of any part of the house. When the Ikards bought the house, the kitchen was down a twisting hall all the way at the back of the house. Two little bedrooms were transformed into this large eat-in kitchen with corner cabinets that hold Jayne's collection of cranberry glass. A fireplace was added, and later the owners discovered old photos of the house showing a chimney on this wall long ago. The kitchen opens onto the dining room through a double doorway affording a view of the harbor from the breakfast table on the far side of the room.*

The turn-of-the-century boat house sits right on the beach. It is
ideal as a place to entertain and also provides endless hours of fun
for grandsons.

TARA-BY-THE-SEA

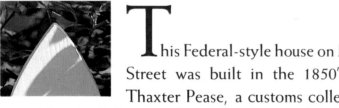

This Federal-style house on North Water Street was built in the 1850's by Joseph Thaxter Pease, a customs collector and the son of Jeremiah Pease, who chose the site for the first camp meeting held in Oak Bluffs. Greg and Gene Sullivan bought the house in 1988 and took it through a total renovation, including the garden. The only things remaining from the old garden are the Belgian-block retaining wall; the hedges; the 'New Dawn' roses, which were overgrown; and grapevines. Gene planned the formal design and chose the plantings—perennials, selected primarily for color and successive seasonal blooms, with some annuals mixed in. Overlooking the ferry to Chappaquiddick, the town dock, and the Inner Harbor, this gracious formal garden with its rose-covered arbor, brick paths, and beds radiating out from a fountain is in its first season at the time of the photograph.

Dwarf boxwood forms a border around each of the four triangular beds, filled with brightly colored dwarf marigolds, petunias, zinnias, and Marguerite daisies. The fountain adds the sound of water to the delicious soft scent of lavender and roses. Privet hedges on two sides of the garden lend an air of grandeur and provide necessary protection from the strong breezes off the harbor. On the right side of the garden is a deep border, filled with a broad variety of perennials, chosen to provide a long season of bloom as well as for color.

In July, this corner of the border features Marguerite daisies (Chrysanthemum frutescens), *yellow yarrow, black-eyed Susans* (Rudbeckia fulgida), *coreopsis* (Coreopsis lanceolata), *liatris* (Liatris spicata), *santolina* (Santolina chamaecyparissus), *lavender* (Lavandula angustifolia), *and blanket flowers* (Gaillardia grandiflora). *Soon, globe thistles* (Echinops ritro) *and painted daisies* (Chrysanthemum coccineum) *will add their blues and reds to the garden when they begin to bloom.*

9 PIERCE'S LANE

This Georgian-style house was built in 1929 for Henry Beetle Hough, editor of *The Vineyard Gazette* for sixty-five years. Keith and Nancy Highet bought the house in 1990 and have renovated and expanded it. On the left is an octagonal library addition. The fanlights over the French doors repeat the design of the original window above the front door. New dormers were added on the third floor. The garage was moved to make room for a guest wing and Nancy's studio next to the kitchen.

On the other side of the house is a new and larger kitchen. The interiors are designed to integrate family antiques and collections with the modern life-style of an active family. Color brings it all together.

Nancy has added extensive gardens, while keeping original plantings of spring bulbs and rhododendrons, bringing them back to life with careful pruning.

Henry Beetle Hough was a staunch defender of the Island's past but he also welcomed well-considered change. Friends feel he would be pleased to see his house today.

ABOVE: *The graceful, curving stone wall outlines the stone terrace outside the library and divides the lawn across the back of the house into two levels, providing for generous perennial borders on the upper level and at the base of the wall as well. The Highets' Corgi, Hotchkiss, is resting on the garden steps.*

OVERLEAF: *The library addition is filled with light from its skylight and the three sets of double French doors. The rug is an early 1900's Oushak from Russian Georgia and was the focus around which Nancy chose colors and other furnishings for the room. The result is an eclectic mixture of old and colorful things.*

LEFT: *The fireplace side of this truncated octagon connects the library to the living room. The fireplace uses the original chimney. Over it, on either side of the mirror, hang two pairs of hand-painted antique maps. On the round table in the foreground is an orchid phalaenopsis.*

FAR LEFT: *A trumpet lamp and a collection of keepsakes, including a marquetry box, a Regency tea caddy, and a sculpted head of the owner's one-week-old daughter are on the table below a map of Virginia in 1585.*

LEFT: *An antique carved German piano stands on the side of the octagon opposite the fireplace wall, in front of a pair of fixed French doors. The painting in the library niche is Dutch; the lamps on either side of the sofa were made from carved wooden dolphin candlesticks.*

RIGHT: *The center hall has been kept very much as it was originally, with its wide pine floorboards, stair rail, and banister. They are original to the house, as is the first door to the living room, seen on the left. The second doorway down was added to balance the space. The wallpaper is from Clarence House. The backdoor leads to the extensive gardens behind the house. The rugs are Chinese needlepoint. The table in the foreground is a nineteenth-century pine half-round that holds a collection of silver boxes and an arrangement from the garden in an Italian vase.*

LEFT: *The kitchen has been completely redone with skylights and large bay windows in the breakfast area.*

BELOW LEFT: *At the front end of the kitchen is a comfortable sitting area. The painting above the wicker sofa is by Nancy Highet. The chest next to the chair was painted by illustrator and artist Margot Datz, who is also Nancy's sister-in-law.*

RIGHT: *The breakfast table is set with French pottery. It is an especially cheerful spot overlooking the lush lawn and gardens in back of the house.*

Architecturally, the living room is very much as it was when the Houghs lived here. A doorway has been added at the end of the hall, the floors pickled, and color added to the room. The dhurrie rug was designed by Nancy, and the watercolor on the wall between the windows is a portrait of her son, Evan. The mantel holds a collection of shells, which decorate the rest of the room as well. Above the mantel is one of several watercolors in the room done by Caribbean artists. To the left of the fireplace wall on the shelves is part of Nancy's collection of blue-and-white Canton china. The fireplace is original to the house and was opened up on the other side to create a fireplace for the library on the same chimney.

THE BACONS

Bright red trim accents the soft gray shingles on the home of Anne and Nathaniel Bacon. Nat, who is a builder by profession, built the house and later added the studio for Anne, who is a floral designer. She created the gardens and many of the design details of the house.

LEFT: *The curving path leads to the front door. A collection of shade-loving plants provides texture. Their various greens mixed with bright yellow daylilies create a cheery welcome.*

RIGHT: *The little birdhouse was designed and constructed by Anne, who cut each of the shingles by hand. A profusion of 'Jackmanii' and 'Romona' clematis climbs up its post.*

FAR RIGHT: *Anne's studio has south-facing windows for plenty of light and winter warmth. Sliding glass doors lead to a deck and garden on the right, where many shade trees outside help cool the studio in summer.*

LEFT: *The nautical aura that permeates this house is continued into the elegant Georgian dining room. The eighteenth-century mahogany Sheraton-style table is encircled with antique copies of Queen Anne chairs and holds pieces of blue-and-white Canton. To the left of the china closet are three of a set of five early nineteenth-century oils of Chinese trading ports. On top of the breakfront is a magnificent model of the Sara E. Newcomb, a Maine coastal schooner typical of the mid- to late-nineteenth century.*

RIGHT: *A little English bachelor's chest, ca. 1730, graces the entrance hall just inside the front door. On the wall leading upstairs are two paintings in primitive style by contemporary American artist Charles Wysocki.*

BELOW: *The Queen Anne tall-case clock, made by Thomas Vernon of English walnut burl, ca. 1708, presides over the hall leading into the dining room and to the outside as well. The wonderful broad moldings are original to the house.*

BELOW: *A brick terrace overlooks the spring gardens. A dogwood (Cornus kousa) outside the back door is just beginning to bloom.*

RIGHT: *Exuberant lilies in many varieties fill the July garden with luscious colors. Bishop's weed (Aegopodium podagraria 'Variegatum') surrounds the pool.*

THE OLSEN HOUSE

One of the first four houses on the street, this house was built in 1837 by Dennis Courtney. Called a three-quarter house, it has two windows on one side of the front door and one window on the other side. The original structure consisted of three main rooms downstairs and one large room upstairs. The kitchen was added around 1875 and the upstairs dormers around 1925. Niels and Eleanor Olsen bought the house in 1964 and took it through extensive renovation, only to have the pipes burst after it was all finished, necessitating further repairs and more renovation.

The house is filled with antiques and art that the Olsens have collected over the years. Many family pieces came from Denmark with Niels and from Kansas, where Eleanor's family were among the early settlers. The end result is this whimsical mixture of furnishings.

ABOVE: *The perfume of this delicate pink climbing rose, which Eleanor brought from her former home in Pelham, New York, scents the air on a clear June morning.*

RIGHT: *A red geranium is the perfect foil for the beautiful patina of the antique copper hanging lantern outside the sitting-room window.*

BELOW: *An 'American Pioneer' climbing rose envelops the bright white fence and trellis in front of the house. Eleanor estimates the rose to be somewhere between fifty and seventy-five years old.*

LEFT: *Victorian in style, the cozy parlor holds an Estee organ, which formerly belonged to a local doctor; he acquired it in exchange for his services. A pair of stately Staffordshire dogs graces the mantel and guards the stern-looking woman in the portrait that Eleanor purports to have rescued from a second-hand store in Pelham, New York. One of a pair, the Windsor armchair has a grip end made to hold a candle or lamp.*

ABOVE: *Sunlight streams through the windows of the cheery parlor, which Eleanor believes may originally have been used as a bedroom. A Victorian loveseat sets the tone for the room. To the left of the window is a grouping of woodcuts by Swedish artist Birger Sandzen, who emigrated to Kansas around 1900 and founded the School of Art at Bethany College. The plant stand beneath the window was made on the Island.*

LEFT: *The striking Italian oval mirror is one of a pair that originally hung in Eleanor's New York office and was presented to her as a retirement gift. She bought the ship painting reflected in the mirror because it reminds her of the pictures of* Old Ironsides *that hung in her schoolroom in Kansas. The little brass lamp to the left of the mirror was originally an oil lamp. The Nantucket basket is by José Formosa Reyes, a well-known basket-maker of the thirties and forties.*

RIGHT: *When the Olsens bought the house in 1964, there was a wood cookstove in the fireplace. The exceptional andirons are pre-Revolutionary and come from a house on the Hudson River. On the mantelpiece, which Niels made, are the powderhorn, gun, and clock case that belonged to Eleanor's great-grandparents and traveled to Kansas with them in a covered wagon. The iron fireplace tools are handmade, and the copper funnel, washtub, charcoal pan, and other items have been collected from various places. On the wall are boat plates from a shipping company and Royal Copenhagen Christmas plates.*

LEFT: *The living room is comfortably furnished with antiques, a Persian rug, and light, bold flower patterns on the chairs and sofa. The oil painting over the sofa is of Monhegan Island, painted by Ray Ellis for his book* North by Northeast. *In the corner between the windows are two oil paintings: The top one is* Haystacks Before the Storm *by Homer Wetson Lewis, painted in the nineteenth century; the lower one is* Sailboats *by Herzog Moore, ca. 1920. To the right of the window is an 1840 linen press.*

RIGHT TOP: *A nineteenth-century painted wooden Balinese wedding horse sits in the corner behind an early-nineteenth-century English mahogany rent table that holds a collection of family photographs.*

RIGHT BOTTOM: *Between the kitchen and master bedroom is a sunny, airy, and cozy den. Over the fireplace is a model of the yacht* America, *for which the America's Cup was named. Over the bedroom door is a half-model of a catboat, and a half-model of a Maine coastal schooner is mounted above the multipaned bow window. On the window shelves in the case is a model of the first Coast Guard cutter, the Harriet Lane.*

FAR LEFT: *A bed of daylilies* (Hemerocallis *hybrids*) *extends nearly the full length of the house.*

LEFT: *In midsummer, the perennial border along the side of the house is filled with black-eyed Susans* (Rudbeckia fulgida), *white* Physostegia virginiana *'Alba' in front of* Eupatorium fistulosum, *stokesia* (Stokesia laevis), *yarrow* (Achillea *hybrid*), *loosestrife* (Lythrum virgatum), *liatris* (Liatris spicata), *astilbe, and baby's breath* (Gypsophila paniculata). *They are underplanted with brightly colored bedding annuals: ageratum, begonias, pink and white alyssum, marigolds, nicotiana, and zinnias.*

BELOW: *The rear exterior view of the house shows part of the low stone wall that surrounds the back lawn. The double doors on the deck open into the dining room. The den is between the main part of the house and the bedroom wing on the right. A bit of the extensive daylily garden can be seen on the right.*

Gleaming terra-cotta tiles from Mexico and deep red walls contribute to the warm mood of the kitchen. Over the butcher-block island in the center of the room is a splendid French brass hanging lamp that was originally an oil lamp. Around the room are more of the Conovers' collection of amusing objects.

ABOVE: *Another English oil painting, this one of ducks, graces the wall behind the counter, which holds a silver tea service, a pair of Staffordshire dogs, a basket of ceramic rolls, and another converted oil lamp with an etched glass shade.*

In comfortable beach-house tradition, the dining room and living room are really one big room with a fireplace at one end. The plain wood walls have been painted with a blue-gray wash, which keeps them from darkening further but maintains their original look and feeling. The furniture in the dining room is mission oak, signed by Stickley. With all its leaves installed, the dining-room table seats twelve comfortably. On the far side of the long room, windowseats hold storage space for firewood. Between the windows, a fold-down desk, made to look like a cupboard when closed, holds old-fashioned games and puzzles and other rainy-day entertainments. The first signal of summer is the family's little bright red Lawley 15, a rare flat-bottomed sailboat that was built in Marblehead and purchased in 1939 from Sherman Hoyt, an America's Cup sailor. Above the pull-down desk is a model of a two-masted schooner—actually a weather vane.

FAR LEFT: *Called the yellow bedroom, even though it is no longer that color, this sunny south room was once a maid's room and, later, Jack's mother's.*

LEFT: *The first-floor bedroom is now the master bedroom and has a wonderful view of the water. Its furnishings have all been in the house since it was built.*

BELOW LEFT AND BELOW: *The east bedroom with its three dormer windows overlooks all the activity of Katama Bay. The red, white, and blue pennants, all named and dated, are sailing prizes of Jack and his brother, Tom. The flag with an anchor is called an Ensign and is traditionally flown from the stern of a sailboat. The origin of the 48-star American flag is not known. The large Japanese flag was picked up by Tom Wuerth from a Japanese submarine beached at Nagasaki after the Armistice in 1945; Tom was task unit commander on a Navy minesweeper that was sent in right after the atomic bomb had been dropped.*

In the heart of the Oak Bluffs Campground, across from Trinity Park, is this lovely little Victorian cottage. The Campground had its beginning in 1835 with the first Methodist camp meeting. Originally it was a true campground with tents, but as the Campground became a permanent fixture, small wooden shelters were built. The cottages themselves began to be built in the 1860's. Oak Bluffs, once known as Cottage City, is one of the first important examples of town planning in the United States. The houses in the Campground are laid out in circular patterns around open park areas. One of these cottages, called Blenheim Minor, belongs to Lucy (Bideau) Hart Abbot, whose great-great-grandfather, Frederick Upham, was the Methodist minister from Edgartown who preached the first camp meeting in Oak Bluffs. After Bideau Abbot bought this cottage and moved in, she discovered that her great-grandfather, also a Methodist preacher, had owned the house next door.

Some three hundred of these Victorian cottages remain out of approximately five hundred that were built. Each one is distinct in its style of Carpenter's Gothic and in its subsequent restorations and renovations. Situated on a corner lot, this cottage was built in 1872 by Joseph Pease, who had had a tent on this location from 1867 to 1872. After Bideau Abbot bought the house in 1986, she made extensive renovations, including winterizing and rewiring. She also enlarged the dining room and music room, and added the solarium, for more light and space. The cottage is furnished with family pieces and memorabilia from Bideau's trips to England.

BELOW: *Blenheim Minor is located on the corner of a row of Victorian cottages, all of which are brightly painted in a variety of colors. Rhododendrons and azaleas decorate the minuscule front yard.*

RIGHT: *The open front door invites visitors into the front parlor, the music room, dining room, and finally the kitchen beyond.*

The dining room and music room are much roomier than they appear from the outside, with space for a grand piano on the left beneath the windows that are part of the extension of this room. The painting next to the piano is of this Campground house and was painted by Bideau's grandson Sixten Abbot. Every bit of space is put to good use, such as the shelf above the dining room that holds some of the owner's many books.

LEFT: *The extra long dining-room table has been in the family for years. Until it was recently refinished, you could see the impressions of Bideau's children's homework in the soft pine finish of the top. The table was originally used for laying out bodies in an undertaker's parlor, or so she was told.*

The pair of finches enjoy the solarium, which was added after Bideau moved in. The cabinet on the wall on the left holds many pieces of family china, which belonged to her grandmother.

RIGHT: *Upstairs under the gabled roof is the cozy front bedroom. A collection of pictures found on trips to Europe, mostly in England, decorates the wall behind the bed.*

This Victorian house, built in 1871, is right on Ocean Park and has a magnificent view of Nantucket Sound beyond the park. In summer its front porches are ideal spots from which to watch band concerts, kite-flying contests, and the fireworks. This section of Oak Bluffs started in the early 1870's as a community of summer homes and hotels. Much younger than Vineyard Haven and Edgartown, Oak Bluffs began as a religious retreat community. As the Campground grew and became more permanent and as people stayed for longer periods than just the camp meetings, shops sprang up along Circuit Avenue. Then hotels and large Victorian summer houses were built overlooking Nantucket Sound and the harbor. Soon the area became a fashionable seaside resort.

Fleming and Henrietta Norris bought their house in 1969 and were summer residents until 1986, when they became year-round residents. When the Norrises first saw the house, it had their main requirements of a view, garden, fireplace, and year-round porches. Even though the interior was painted in dark colors, it was love at first sight, and after only a few minutes of looking, they bought the house.

RIGHT: *The downstairs porch wraps around the whole front of the house. It faces east and therefore is shady in the afternoon and captures the breezes from the Sound. The windows seen at the top of the porch open from the bottom up and are raised by cords and pulleys secured on latches at the porch supports.*

LEFT: *The upstairs guest bedroom with its sunny fabrics and white walls has photos of the couple's son and his family. This inviting room opens out onto the shady upstairs porch, which stretches across the whole front of the second floor.*

BELOW: *The upstairs bedroom and dressing room have been redone into a luxurious masterpiece of color, complete with Jacuzzi, TV, and an intercom.*

LEFT: *The long perennial border extends the length of the property. Blooming here in late summer are white* Echinaecea purpurea, *white phlox* (Phlox paniculata), *and* Rudbeckia, *backed by crimson and white rose of sharon and interspersed with annuals, for color. A garden rich in color, there is something in bloom from spring until fall.*

RIGHT: *The West Chop lighthouse.*

LEFT: *Mountain laurel* (Kalmia latifolia *'Ostbo Red'*) *blossoms.* ABOVE: *When the garage was added, its location led to the brick circle garden and the "little secret garden" next to the garage with its wisteria-covered entrance.* 'Betty Prior' *roses grow along the garage wall.* BELOW LEFT: *A Chinese dogwood* (Cornus kousa) *is in full bloom to the right of Kalmia latifolia* 'Ostbo Red' *with a low bird's nest spruce in front of it.* BELOW AND RIGHT: *The red of a cut-leaf Japanese maple* (Acer palmatum *'Everred dissectum'*) *dominates the lily pond. In addition to the water lilies in the water garden itself are tall horsetail grass* (Equisetum hyemale) *and Umbrella palm* (Cyperus alternifolius). *To left of the maple is a bright white climbing clematis. Cotoneaster* (Cotoneaster horizontalis) *and flowering thyme* (Thymus vulgaris) *provide interest as ground covers between the rocks and the bricks.*

LEFT: *The outside of the old water tower is now the wall between the kitchen and living room. The original structure was painted in a red and white checked pattern. When Broni began to plane down the old boards, he decided he liked the effect of the old paint and kept the look. A fireplace has been set into the wall behind the stairs.*

BELOW AND RIGHT: *Broni's studio. Outside the door is a dark pink rambling rose the Lesnikowskis named Grandmother Berry's rose because it was started from a slip taken from Annie's grandmother's rose in Kentucky. It originally came with her family from England in the 1600's, first to North Carolina and then Kentucky.*

The first studio was reconstructed from an old horse barn that Broni bought for $80 and moved to this site from Gay Head. It burned down and had to be built again. He designed the interior without cross ties so that large work can be moved around. Extremely complicated to frame, the central truss stabilizes the building and eliminates the need for collar ties. The rafters support the structure. He built the studio to give him both height and light. The large bay window at the end overlooks the Lagoon.

Broni's workbench in his studio, showing some of his wood carving in progress and "an accumulation of things that interest me."

The large border is planted with tall perennials such as hydrangeas, 'Fairy' roses, phlox, lythrum, and daylilies. In the middle height range are daisies, coreopsis, coneflowers, peonies, liatris, lupines, globe thistles, chrysanthemums, and poppies. Lower-growing plants are a combination of annuals (alyssum, petunias, candytuft, snapdragons, and zinnias) and perennials (leadwort, coral bells, dianthus, and primroses) to complete the color palette of seasonal blooms.

Seen in detail from left to right are: bee balm, phlox, lily, daylily, and hydrangea.

LEFT: *The armchair dates from 1808, when it was made for the daughter of William Ellery, a signer of the Declaration of Independence, upon her marriage. The oil portrait over the mantel is of the ship Dolphin, ca. 1800.*

ABOVE: *On the intricately carved mantelpiece is a tapestry, woven by one of the Hales' daughters, depicting a bird's-eye view of the Vineyard with the family's favorite spots, boats, and horses carefully included.*

RIGHT: *The Hales' cat, Spice, sits in front of a border of foxglove (Digitalis purpurea), English daisies (Bellis perennis), and striped grass (Miscanthus sinensis 'Zebrinus') backed by a golden rain tree (Koelreuteria paniculata), a Chinese dogwood (Cornus kousa 'Seven Stars'), and a Colorado blue spruce (Picea pungens glauca).*

Some 60 feet in diameter, this stone-walled garden has four concentric circles around a flagstone terrace, 7 feet in diameter. Perennials fill the outer ring and provide interest year-round with textures and foliage colors. The two inner circles are planted with annuals, arranged by color; the center ring with culinary and decorative herbs is edged with a santolina border. A curving brick walk leads to the center. Located some distance from the house on a lower lawn, the garden is planted so that, when viewed from the house, the soft pastels of roses and other perennials evolve into bolder colors of annuals and perennials chosen for the inner circles and the far side of the perennial border.

LEFT: *In late June, bold colors are predominant on this side of the garden as seen from the stables. Blooming in the perennial ring are* Monarda didyma *'Cambridge Scarlet',* Lychnis coronaria, Gaillardia aristata *'Dazzler', and* Coreopsis grandiflora *'Early Sunrise'. Masses of peppermint (*Mentha pererita*) hug the low stone wall and 'Cherry Rose' nasturtiums tumble over it.*

BELOW: *On either side of the steps that lead into the garden are lavender (*Lavandula angustifolia*),* Teucrium chamaedrys, *and catmint (*Nepeta faassenii *'Blue Wonder'). Their gray and silver foliage balances the pale pink 'Fairy' roses behind. To the right of the steps are ox-eye daisies (*Chrysanthemum leucanthemum*), part of the plantings that are repeated throughout the border and span the season with blooms.*

Inside the former barn is a beautiful home filled with collections of ship models, ship paintings, and other Island art. Outside the deck doors is Lake Tashmoo. The living room is filled with light from the large windows and two pairs of glass doors. A model of Pat's Friendship sloop Erda, named for their daughter's first operatic role, was built by Pat and his son, Nathaniel. On the wall above the fireplace is an oil painting of the schooner America as rerigged by owner F. L. Barnum. Between the fireplace and the door to the deck is an oil painting of the herring fleet and smokehouses in Bourneholme, Denmark, painted by Matthew Geddes, a Danish artist who painted in Menemsha. RIGHT: The view looking toward the front hall and stairs shows the level of the old hayloft in the house's former incarnation as a barn. On the wall above and between the two white doors hangs a portrait of Pat's father, Francis West, painted by his good friend Jim Gilbert, an artist and naturalist from Chilmark.

THE BARN

Katharine Cornell acquired this old Vineyard barn because she wanted to keep her own cow and needed a place for it. Nancy Hamilton, who was Katharine Cornell's secretary as well as a composer and scriptwriter, acquired the barn and renovated it into a house in 1959. Many additions have been made to the structure, which is on the wooded western shore of Lake Tashmoo, a tidal pond that opens into Vineyard Sound.

After Katharine Cornell's husband died, the actress sold her large house nearby and moved here, where she spent the rest of her days. The house is filled with an amazing collection of furnishings and memorabilia. Margaret Lindsay purchased The Barn in 1989 and has carefully preserved its spaces with as many of Katharine Cornell's furnishings as possible.

ABOVE: *The rambling house as seen from the marsh on the water side of the property. The two-story section adjoining the large screened porch is the original barn and comprises the living and dining rooms and the upstairs bedroom. Several bedroom suites on the right are joined to the barn by a modern kitchen–breakfast room area.*

RIGHT: *The multipaned windows with objects from a glass collection displayed on the partitions are part of the kitchen wing. The front door opens into a little entrance hall and then the dining room.*

VICTORIAN GARDEN

A garden restoration began when this 1890's house was bought by Dale and Frank Loy in 1979. Remnants of a once grand garden were present in an inner garden that had been a croquet lawn with a formal border. It had become little more than a tangle of weeds. In an upper garden, utilitarian beds for berries, vegetables, and flowers have been redone into cutting gardens for herbs, salad greens, and flowers for the house.

Recovering the garden area meant pulling out all the ivy, myrtle, and sweet peas that had taken over. Then any surviving perennials were lifted and the soil was replaced with new topsoil, seaweed, and manure. A wooden barrier to keep the vines from intruding from the soil level, or at least slow them down, was installed. The surviving perennials, such as *Physostegia virginiana*, lupines, and wild sweet peas (*Lathyrus odoratus*), were then regrouped and replanted with additional old-fashioned flowers such as single hollyhocks (*Althaea rosea*), astilbe, Shasta daisies (*Chrysanthemum* x *superbum*), *Phlox paniculata*, daylilies (*Hemerocallis* hybrids), perennial geranium (*Geranium endressi*), lamb's ears (*Stachys byzantina*), columbine (*Aquilegia* hybrids), Oriental lilies, *Lobelia siphilitica*, *Lychnis coronaria*, liatris (*Liatris spicata*), *Salvia* x *superba* 'East Friesland', and stokesia (*Stokesia laevis*). Black-eyed Susans (*Rudbeckia hirta*) and sweet Williams reseed themselves from year to year.

UP-ISLAND

ABOVE: *Mexican terra-cotta tiles add warmth to the living area of the barn, furnished with an interesting mix of antiques such as a Brittany bed that functions as a hutch.* RIGHT: *The kitchen window overlooks a wildflower meadow, stone walls, and fields beyond.* BELOW: *A photograph by Raymond Kellman, taken in Yugoslavia, on the wall above an old painted chest from Durango, Mexico.*

LEFT: *An upstairs shower is brightly lit by its pyramidal skylight.*

BELOW LEFT: *The coziness of this small bedroom is enhanced by the deck on the far end of the room and the light from skylights overhead, which also allow a view of the stars at night.*

RIGHT: *Sunny and cheery, the master bedroom with its large sun deck is beautiful at sunrise, when the Elizabeth Islands across the Sound glow pink in the early-morning light. The fireplace was designed and built by the LaRhettes' architect.*

MIDDEN MOOR

When the owners bought the property some thirty years ago, it was moorland, broken up with eighteenth-century stone walls, overlooking Menemsha Pond. They built the house to take advantage of the magnificent views. English-style dooryard gardens have been meticulously planted and maintained near the house, and the wild beauty of the surrounding moors encloses the property on all sides.

The living room with its interesting arrangement of windows for light and views of the sea has a deep marble fireplace and recessed shelves that provide ample space for the owners to display some of their collection of contemporary American ceramics. The globes in the foreground are antique American pieces. Two Danish oil-on-wood paintings of Viking ships hang over the fireplace.

SOURCES

ARCHITECTS

Robert Avakian, page 97
Arthur Cogswell, pages 206–211
Joseph L. Eldredge, pages 18–23, 66–67, 198–
    205, 228–231, 232–236, 276
Steven Holl, pages 254–257
Eliot Noyes, pages 237–241
Frederick Noyes, pages 223–225
Geoffrey White, pages 213–219

DECORATIVE PAINTING

Margot Datz, pages 4, 6
Mary Mayhew, page 9
Stanley Murphy, pages 160, 161

FLOWER ARRANGEMENTS

Anne Bacon, pages 43, 248, 250, 251
Alison Cannon, pages 44–51
Teddie Ellis, pages 60–69
Catherine Fallin, pages 60–63, 76–77, 80, 83–
    89, 160–163, 256–257
Liz Gude, pages 182–191
Anne Hale, pages 124–131
Mariko Kawaguchi, pages 90–97
Eleanor Hubbard, pages 212–219
Julia Mitchell, pages 260–265
Eleanor Olsen, pages 52–59
Jacqueline Ronan, pages 2–13
Sara Jane Sylvia, pages 170–179
Margaret Koski Schwier, pages 11, 19–23,
    150–153
Trudy Taylor, page 211
Isabel West, pages 140–243

GARDEN CONSULTANTS

Anne Bacon
Marion Baker
Margaret Koski Schwier

HORTICULTURALIST

Polly Hill, pages 266–269

INTERIOR DESIGNER

Leta A. Foster, pages 98–107

HORTICULTURAL STYLING

Donorama Nurseries, pages 90–97
Mariko Kawaguchi, pages 96–97

LANDSCAPE ARCHITECTS/DESIGNERS

Anne Hale, pages 124–131, 198–205
Rebecca Potter, pages 108–111
Maurice Wrangell, pages 244–253

LANDSCAPE GARDENERS

Michael Faracca, pages 24–27
John Gadowski, pages 108–111
Virginia Iverson, pages 108–111
Carlos Montoya, pages 220–221
Margaret Koski Schwier, pages 18–23, 132–
    135, 144–147, 168–169, 258–259
Nina Schneider, pages 192–197
Chuck Wiley, pages 96–97

**SELECTED GARDEN AND HISTORICAL
REFERENCES**

Bloom, Alan. *Alpines for Your Garden*. Chicago:
    Floraprint, U.S.A., 1981.
Damrosch, Barbara. *The Garden Primer*. New
    York: Workman Publishing Company,
    Inc., 1988.
Foley, Daniel J. *Gardening by the Sea, from Coast
    to Coast*. Orleans, Mass.: Parnassus, 1982.
Hale, Anne. *Moraine to Marsh, a Field Guide to
    Martha's Vineyard*. Vineyard Haven, Mass.:
    Watership Gardens, 1988.
Hough, Henry Beetle and Alfred Eisenstaedt.
    Martha's Vineyard. New York: The Viking
    Press, 1970.
Huntington, Gale. *Introduction to Martha's Vine-
    yard*. Edgartown, Mass.: Dukes County
    Historical Society, 1969.
McAlester, A. Lee and Virginia McAlester. *A
    Field Guide to American Houses*. New York:
    Alfred A. Knopf, 1984.

Macy, Eliot Eldridge. *The Captain's Daughters of
    Martha's Vineyard*. The Chatham Press,
    1978.
Nerney, Ruth S. *Reflections in Crystal Lake, East
    Chop, Martha's Vineyard*. 1985.
Niering, William A. and Nancy C. Olmstead.
    *The Audubon Society Field Guide to North Amer-
    ican Wildflowers, Eastern Region*. New York:
    Alfred A. Knopf, 1979.
Norton, James. *A Walking Tour of William Street*.
    Edgartown, Mass.: Dukes County Histori-
    cal Society, 1985.
Railton, Arthur R. *Walking Tour of Historic Edgar-
    town*. Edgartown, Mass.: Dukes County
    Historical Society, 1988.
Stoddard, Chris. *A Centennial History of Cottage
    City*. Oak Bluffs, Mass.: Oak Bluffs Histor-
    ical Commission.
Taylor, Norman. *Taylor's Guide to Annuals*. Bos-
    ton: Houghton Mifflin Company, 1961.
————. *Taylor's Guide to Shrubs*. Boston: Hough-
    ton Mifflin Company, 1987.
Weiss, Ellen. *City in the Woods: The Life and De-
    sign of an American Camp Meeting on Martha's
    Vineyard*. New York: Oxford University
    Press, 1987.
West, Isabel White. *Wilfred O. White, 1878–
    1955, a Family Journal*. Vineyard Haven,
    Mass.: 1990.
White Flower Farms. *The Garden Book Catalog*.
    Spring 1991. Litchfield, Conn.

PRODUCTION CREDITS

Design concept and photo layouts by Taylor
    Lewis
Type design and mechanicals by Abby Kagan
Photography assistance by Greg Hadley and
    Greg Goebel
Editorial production by Pamela Stinson and
    Susan Groarke
Copy edited by Marion Baker and Kate Scott
Proofread by Susan Groarke and Pauline
    Piekarz
Composition by N.K. Graphics
Production coordination by Joanne Barracca
Printed and bound by Tien Wah Press